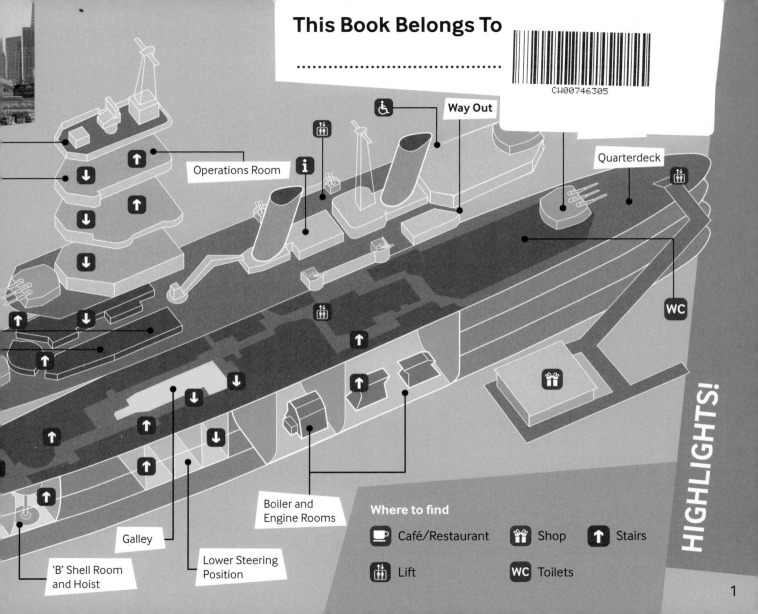

This Book Belongs To

....

CW00746305

Way Out

Operations Room

Quarterdeck

'B' Shell Room and Hoist

Galley

Lower Steering Position

Boiler and Engine Rooms

WC

Where to find

☕ Café/Restaurant   🎁 Shop   ⬆ Stairs

🛗 Lift   WC Toilets

HIGHLIGHTS!

1

WELCOME

Welcome aboard HMS *Belfast!*

This is the last surviving British big-gun warship from the middle of the twentieth century, when Britain's power and wealth came from its Empire, protected by the Royal Navy.

HMS *Belfast* served for 25 years. The ship and its crew travelled the world, fighting in famous actions in the Second World War and in the Korean War in the 1950s. You will learn about these and other stories, about how the ship worked and what life was like on board for the crew.

HMS *Belfast* has nine different levels, with countless ladders taking you up and down the decks to different parts of the ship. It is easy to get lost as you explore, so stick with your group and enjoy making unexpected discoveries.

Be careful as you move around the ship: there are tight spaces and lots of ladders.

WARNING

The ship's hull is divided into watertight compartments so that damage in one place would not flood the whole ship. This makes it impossible to walk along the lower decks without going up and down ladders. Make sure you face each ladder as you climb up or down.

Hatches (doorways) on board often have raised ledges to stop water moving around the ship. Mind your head and feet whenever you go through a hatch to avoid bashing your shins — sailors called this 'hatch rash'.

Look out for:

- The 'Find It' tag, which shows you special things to look out for on your visit

FIND IT!

- Sticker activities, which use the stickers at the back of this book

STICKER IT!

- 'Start a Conversation': questions to get you talking with your family about what you have seen

Start a Conversation

- 'Fun Facts' to boggle your mind

Fun Fact

- Quotes telling the stories of HMS *Belfast* in the words of people who were there

- Activities to do either during your visit or later on at home

ACTIVITY

CONTENTS

STEP ABOARD

HMS *Belfast* was built in 1938, a time when many countries were building new warships. Britain's navy had been the strongest in the world for most of the last hundred years and aimed to stay that way, in spite of threats from countries including Japan and Germany. HMS *Belfast* is a cruiser, a type of ship that combines the advantages of speed, range and powerful guns. It was designed to be able to travel the world and protect the British Empire, including its trading ships.

The Quarterdeck is the first part of the ship that you see when you step on board. It was a special area, usually reserved for officers. Religious services were often held here.

The White Ensign is the flag of a Royal Navy ship. HMS *Belfast* no longer serves in the Royal Navy, but has special permission to fly the White Ensign every day.

At the commissioning ceremony when HMS *Belfast* officially became a Royal Navy ship, the civilian Red Ensign flag had to be swapped for the White Ensign. There was a problem though: the Red Ensign got tangled around the pole, so the ceremony had to wait while a sailor climbed up to get it.

STOP

The deck here is wooden, as it would have been in the 1930s when the ship was first built. A metal strip on the deck marks the edge of the Quarterdeck. Ratings (sailors who were not officers) needed a reason to cross this line.

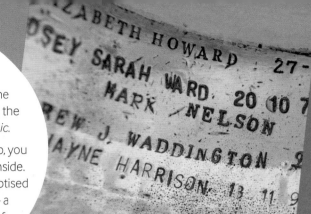

FIND IT!

Look for the silver bell, a gift from the city of Belfast where the ship was built. The shipbuilders were Harland and Wolff, the same company that built the *Titanic*.

If you stand under the bell and look up, you can see names and dates engraved inside. These record the babies who were baptised using the upturned bell as a font – a special privilege for the children of HMS *Belfast*'s officers.

The bell on board ship was used to tell the time, like in some schools. Instead of lessons, each day and night were divided into different 'watches'. The bell rang to mark every hour of each watch. Sailors worked and rested in shifts according to the watches.

HMS *Belfast*'s crest shows a sea horse, as does the crest of the city of Belfast.

Second dog watch: 6pm – 8pm

First watch: 8pm – midnight

First dog watch: 4pm – 6pm

Afternoon watch: noon – 4pm

Middle watch: midnight – 4am

Forenoon watch: 8am – noon

Morning watch: 4am – 8am

STEP ABOARD

5

LEARN THE ROPES

Hundreds of sailors at a time lived and worked on board HMS *Belfast* – at its busiest the ship was home to nearly a thousand men. Life on board ship was run according to Royal Navy rules and timetables. 'Learning the ropes' comes from the days of sailing ships, when sailors had to know all the ropes and sails on board. By the twentieth century the 'ropes' that new recruits needed to learn included new skills, new habits and even new words.

Members of the crew exchange uniforms in a Christmas tradition, Christmas Day 1942.

> *'I think the happiest ship I ever served in was the* Belfast.'
> Kenneth Arthur Etheridge, Master-at-Arms in HMS *Belfast* 1960–62

The key to being a 'happy ship' was a disciplined crew, well led by the Captain. The crew trained and practised activities constantly until they worked together as smoothly as a machine. There were strict rules for everything – you even needed permission to grow a beard.

Each person on board had their own place in the pecking order. This status was known as your rank (for officers) or rate (non-officers), and it ran from Senior Officers down to Boy Seamen. Each member of the crew could tell from another person's uniform and badges whether they ranked above or below him. Most of the sailors on board were ratings; they did the everyday work on board and were led by the officers. The Captain was in charge of the ship.

The youngest members of the crew were the Boy Seamen. Brian Butler (above left) joined HMS *Belfast* as a Boy Seaman at the age of 16 during the Second World War.

Fun Fact

He, She, It

All the sailors in HMS *Belfast*'s crew were male. According to an old tradition, they called the ship itself 'she'. These days we often use 'it' for a ship instead, but you may see and hear both.

To help you find your way around, learn these words for the parts of a ship:

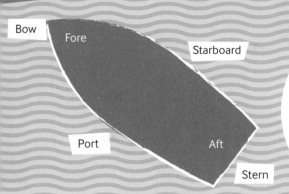

Bow · Fore · Starboard · Port · Aft · Stern

FIND IT!

There are codes like this one on the hatches (doors) all around HMS *Belfast*. The codes told sailors where they were on board ship. There were numbers for the different decks, while letters from A to Z pinpointed areas from the bow to the stern.

Z

2N PT AFT

ACTIVITY

JACKSPEAK

Life in the Royal Navy came with a whole new language to learn: Jackspeak, or sailors' slang. See if you can pair up the Jackspeak in the left-hand column with the English translation on the right.

heads
oggin
agony bags
nutty
bucket of fog
jack
pot mess
cackleberries

the sea
eggs
stew
toilets
bagpipes
chocolate
a confused situation
a Royal Navy sailor

heads – toilets; oggin – the sea; agony bags – bagpipes; nutty – chocolate; bucket of fog – a confused situation; Jack – a Royal Navy sailor; pot mess – stew; cackleberries – eggs

7

SECOND WORLD WAR 1939–1945

Just a few weeks after HMS *Belfast* was commissioned, the Second World War began.

HMS *Belfast* patrolled the northern seas to stop supplies being taken to and from Britain's enemies in Germany. It was part of the Royal Navy's Northern Patrol which stopped and checked ships in the seas around Scotland, Norway, Denmark, Iceland and Greenland. In October 1939 HMS *Belfast* captured a German ship called the *Cap Norte* which was in disguise, painted with a different name and flying the Swedish flag.

HMS *Belfast* had two Walruses on board. A 'Walrus' was a type of aircraft, used for observation and to look for enemy ships and submarines. There was no space on board for a runway, so the planes were launched using a catapult which shot them off the side of the ship. The Walruses landed at sea. They were then lifted back on deck using the ship's cranes.

This photo shows a Walrus launching from HMS *Mauritius*, also a light cruiser in the Royal Navy.

EXPLOSION AT SEA, NOVEMBER 1939

NOVEMBER 1939, OFF THE COAST OF SCOTLAND: JOHN HARRISON WAS ON DUTY INSIDE A GUN TURRET. THERE WAS NO SIGN OF ANY THREAT.

SUDDENLY A MAGNETIC MINE EXPLODED RIGHT UNDER THE SHIP.

THE EXPLOSION KNOCKED HMS *BELFAST*'S ELECTRICAL GENERATORS OUT OF PLACE AND THE LIGHTS WENT OUT.

'I FELT MY SPINE GOING UP INTO MY SKULL AND EVERYTHING WENT DARK – THEN IT WAS DEAD SILENCE, FOLLOWED BY A SHAKING UP AND DOWN.'

JOHN OPENED THE HATCH TO ESCAPE, BUT WATER RUSHED IN. HE FEARED THE SHIP WAS SINKING. LUCKILY IT WAS JUST A BROKEN PIPE.

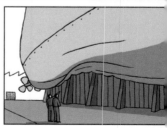

THE EXPLOSION DAMAGED HMS *BELFAST*'S HULL, SMASHED THE ENGINE ROOMS AND KNOCKED THE GUN TURRETS OUT OF PLACE.

TWENTY CREW MEMBERS WERE INJURED AND ONE MAN DIED. IT COULD EASILY HAVE BEEN WORSE. THE SHIP WAS SO BADLY DAMAGED THAT IT TOOK THREE YEARS TO REPAIR.

This torpedo is kept in a part of HMS *Belfast* that used to be an open deck. From there torpedoes like this were fired out to sea at enemy ships. Once the torpedo was underwater, it was ready to explode when it hit the target.

Torpedoes fired by German submarines, or U-boats, were a serious threat to Royal Navy ships. In October 1939 HMS *Royal Oak*, a British battleship, was sunk by a torpedo while anchored near HMS *Belfast* in Scapa Flow in the Orkney Islands. Two-thirds of the crew were killed.

The damage caused to HMS *Belfast* by the mine in 1939 was extremely serious. The ship had to be almost completely rebuilt, which gave engineers a chance to fit it with the latest technology. In 1942 HMS *Belfast* was back in action, a very different ship than at the start of the war.

- The armoured 'belt' protecting the middle of the hull was enlarged and extended
- The latest radar was added to locate the enemy, replacing the Walrus planes
- The latest automatic fire control system was added, using radar to help to aim and fire the guns
- More and better anti-aircraft guns were added
- The hull was painted in 'Dazzle' camouflage patterns to confuse enemy submarines which might attack the ship

HMS *Belfast* steams towards D-Day, June 1944.

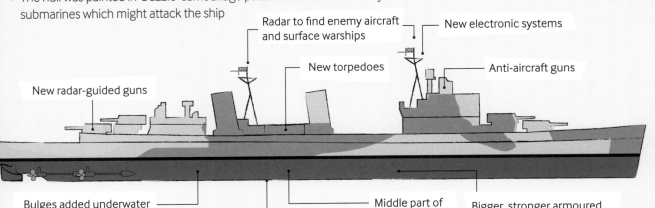

Radar to find enemy aircraft and surface warships

New electronic systems

New torpedoes

Anti-aircraft guns

New radar-guided guns

Bulges added underwater for increased stability

Broken 'spine' of the ship repaired. The spine is referred to as the 'keel'.

Middle part of the ship rebuilt

Bigger, stronger armoured belt fixed around the middle of the hull

ARCTIC CONVOYS

From 1941 Britain sent supplies by sea to its allies in the Soviet Union in groups of ships known as the Arctic Convoys. German ships, submarines and aircraft often attacked these convoys, so Royal Navy ships escorted them. It was a dangerous mission, in freezing weather, darkness and waves sometimes higher than the ships. Prime Minister Winston Churchill called the Arctic Convoys 'the worst journey in the world'.

In 1943 HMS *Belfast* joined the Arctic Convoys to guard the merchant ships that carried vital supplies.

The Arctic Messdeck on board HMS *Belfast* shows how the crew lived, slept and ate in Messdecks like these during months at sea with the Arctic Convoys.

Ice built up quickly on top of the ship and its weight could be dangerous. The crew had to hack ice off the decks by hand to stop the ship from tipping over.

Able Seaman Thomas B Day standing against the ice encrusted barbette for 'B' Turret on board HMS *Belfast*, 1943.

Ice forming on the fo'c'sle and 'A' and 'B' Turrets of HMS *Belfast*, 1943.

To avoid being seen, the convoys travelled in winter, when daylight in the Arctic only lasts for an hour or two. Moving around the icy decks in darkness was difficult and dangerous. It was so cold that if you touched metal with your bare hand, your skin would freeze to it.

Seamen clearing ice from the fo'c'sle of HMS *Belfast*, November 1943.

Fun Fact

A reindeer travelled on HMS *Belfast* for a while in 1943. She was a thank you present from a Soviet Admiral to the British Vice-Admiral. The crew looked after her in a hangar which had been home to a Walrus seaplane.

HMS Belfast in Action against the Scharnhorst, 26 December 1943, a painting by John Hamilton.

In late December 1943 HMS *Belfast* was getting ready to escort a convoy home from the Soviet Union. A message came for HMS *Belfast*'s commander to say that a feared German battleship, the *Scharnhorst*, was coming to attack them. This was a rare chance to take on the famous enemy ship and make all the Arctic Convoys safer. Together with other Royal Navy ships, HMS *Belfast* chased down the *Scharnhorst* off the north coast of Norway and helped to attack and sink it.

'*I had no other feeling than pity for several minutes ... I don't think I felt like cheering ... the job had been accomplished.*'
Lieutenant-Commander Charles Simpson

'*There was a wonderful firework display on the horizon. The commander over the loudspeakers told us the bearings of the* Scharnhorst *and the* Duke of York *and we watched the battle. You could see a great red flash, and then the great salvos of tracer shells going slowly over in a great arc. It was extraordinary.*'
Ordinary Seaman John Wilson

The *Scharnhorst* sank and the battle was won. But instead of joy, many of HMS *Belfast*'s crew felt sympathy for the German sailors. The losses were terrible: only 36 men survived from the *Scharnhorst*'s crew of nearly 2,000.

ARCTIC CONVOYS

HOW TO SAIL A WARSHIP

Sailing a warship such as HMS *Belfast* needed both advanced technology and highly skilled people – not to mention a lot of fuel oil. Teams worked together from the top to the bottom of the ship to turn the officers' commands into movement.

FIND IT!

Changes of speed were communicated through the ship using engine telegraphs like this.

Fun Fact

HMS *Belfast's* top speed was 32 knots (about 36 miles per hour). The word 'knots' comes from the old way of measuring a ship's speed. Sailors tied a log on to the end of a knotted rope, then threw it overboard. They counted how many knots passed in a minute.

5 Propellers
Engineers in the Engine Rooms follow orders from the engine telegraphs to change the speed of the engines powering the propellers. This changes the ship's speed.

4 Rudder
Pressure in the pipes turns the rudder to steer the ship in the right direction.

3 Pipes
When the Helmsman turns the wheel a change in pressure passes along hydraulic pipes to the rear of the ship

The power to move the 12,000-ton HMS *Belfast* through the water came from its boilers and engines. Down in the bottom of the hull there were four boilers and four engines. These could be used in different combinations as needed.

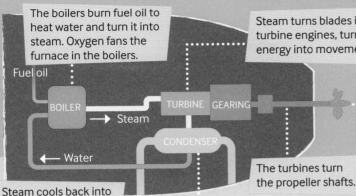

The boilers burn fuel oil to heat water and turn it into steam. Oxygen fans the furnace in the boilers.

Steam turns blades in the turbine engines, turning heat energy into movement energy.

Fuel oil

BOILER

→ Steam

TURBINE | GEARING

CONDENSER

← Water

The propellers, also known as 'screws' in ships, turn to move the ship through the water.

The turbines turn the propeller shafts.

Steam cools back into water in the condenser.

The Boiler and Engine Rooms (above) are the powerhouse of the ship. Right down in the bottom of the hull, they are a maze of pipes, valves and ladders. Check the height chart on board to make sure you are tall enough to explore them safely.

1 Bridge
Officers send steering and speed orders to the Helmsman.

2 Lower steering position
The Helmsman turns the ship's wheel to change the angle of the rudder. He also uses the engine telegraphs to change the speed and direction of the engines. Deep inside the ship, the Helmsman relies on orders and cannot see where he is going.

HOW TO SAIL A WARSHIP

13

D-DAY 1944

In June 1944 the Allies began the fight to free the countries in Europe which were controlled by Nazi Germany. The operation, known as 'D-Day', began on 6 June. The navies, armies and air forces of Britain, the USA, Canada and other allies worked together to land tens of thousands of soldiers on beaches in Normandy, France. HMS *Belfast* supported the landings by firing on German defences to clear the way for the Allied soldiers.

ACTIVITY

WARTIME DANGERS

Follow the trails to find out how to protect the ship from each Second World War threat.

 Torpedo boats

  Submarines

 Mines

Aircraft

Locate them using ASDIC sonar equipment

Use the 'degaussing' process to make the ship less magnetic

 Fire 4-inch guns

IN ACTION ON D-DAY, 1944

RIVER CLYDE

JUNE 1944: HMS *BELFAST* LEFT SCOTLAND AND SAILED SOUTH TO SUPPORT ALLIED FORCES IN THE NORMANDY LANDINGS.

YOU COULD HAVE WALKED ACROSS TO FRANCE ON SHIPS AND LANDING CRAFT!

THE CHANNEL WAS FULL OF THOUSANDS OF SHIPS - THIS WAS THE LARGEST EVER LANDING OF SOLDIERS BY SEA.

I WOULDN'T BE A SOLDIER

HMS *BELFAST*'S CREW WAVED TO SOLDIERS HEADING FOR THE BEACHES ON THE ROUGH SEA. THEY WERE COLD, TIRED, SCARED AND SEASICK.

HMS *BELFAST* FIRED AT THE GERMAN GUNS ON SHORE TO HELP ALLIED TROOPS. THE LIBERATION OF FRANCE HAD BEGUN AND HMS *BELFAST* HAD LED THE WAY.

HMS *Belfast*'s guns played a vital role on D-Day, and in the days and weeks after the first landings.

1 The Bridge and the Gunnery Control Tower
Officers decide which targets to fire on. Lookouts help to gather information about a target's location, movement and speed. This information is sent down to the Transmitting Station.

To fire HMS *Belfast*'s main guns, crew members in different parts of the ship had to calculate precisely how to aim them, then send that information to the people aiming the guns. The ammunition for the main guns was kept deep inside the ship.

4 Gun Turret
Gun crews load and aim the guns. One of the seven members of the gun team then presses the firing button.

2 Transmitting Station
Using all the data, including weather conditions and HMS *Belfast*'s speed, Royal Marines calculate exactly where to aim the guns and send orders to the Gun Turret crew.

3 Shell Room and Cordite Room
Shells and cordite (propellent) are sent up hoists to the Gun Turrets.

Fun Fact

HMS *Belfast*'s biggest weapons are '6-inch' guns — the diameter of the shells they fired. Shells from the ship's main guns could reach targets up to 14 miles away.

'It wasn't a very nice thing to see, lives being wasted. Doesn't matter whether you're German or British or what you are, it's not nice.'
Gunner Denis Watkinson on learning that HMS *Belfast*'s guns had destroyed a German gun position and only one enemy soldier had survived.

D-DAY 1944

15

THE FLOATING TOWN

As well as being a warship, HMS *Belfast* was a home from home for months at a time to the hundreds of men who made up its crew. It also acted as a 'mothership', supporting sailors on smaller ships and even soldiers fighting nearby. The ship had everything its crew needed: a shop, a laundry, a chapel, a mail room, a sick bay and workshops for engineering and sewing, as well as places to store and cook food for everyone on board. HMS *Belfast* was a whole floating town.

'It was very, very comfortable, extremely comfortable to sleep in. You were really snug.'
Boy Seaman Brian Butler

During the Second World War, sailors slept in hammocks in their Messdecks. The hammocks were packed away in daytime. When fixed bunks were introduced, some of the crew missed the comfort of a cosy hammock.

Charles Simpson watched another ship sink after being hit by a mine in 1944. He remembered later how sad he felt. *'When you see a ship gradually sink beneath the waves, you think of a sailor's home being destroyed.'*
Lieutenant-Commander Charles Simpson

Sailors of HMS *Belfast* with a young cat, possibly named 'Frankenstein'.

Start a Conversation

With not much space in the Messdecks, sailors had small 'ditty boxes' in which to pack their personal belongings while they were at sea. What would you take with you?

The ship's cats had a job to do, keeping rats and mice out of the food stores, but they were also well-loved pets. You can even buy your own 'Frankenstein' soft toy in the Shop.

HMS *Belfast*'s Sick Bay was big enough for minor operations. The crew were treated here; so were injured soldiers and civilians brought on board for treatment at D-Day and during the Korean War. Prisoners who had been fighting against the British were also given medical care on board. There was even a dental surgery.

Fun Fact

Action Stations!
As well as their regular job, everyone on board had a particular place and duty which they had to get to in a hurry when the 'Action Stations' alarm sounded. Victor Padbury was usually a Baker on board, but his Action Station was deep inside the ship, sending explosive cordite up to the Gun Turrets.

ACTIVITY

CHOOSE YOUR JOB

There are so many different jobs to be done on board ship – which one would suit you best? Answer the questions to find out.

Do you like making things?

- Nothing better → **How are you in the early mornings?**
  - Brilliant → **Baker**
  - Bleary → **Which craft would you rather learn?**
    - Woodwork → **Shipwright**
    - Sewing → **Sailmaker**
- It's not my favourite → **Would you like to do a desk job?**
  - Sounds awful → **Are you better with machines or people?**
    - Machines — I'm great with tech → **Engineer**
    - People — I'm a born leader → **Captain**
  - Yes please → **ASDIC operator**

ASDIC operator
Pay close attention as you listen for the 'pings' that might warn of nearby submarines.

Baker
Get kneading: the bakery can make 50 loaves of bread every day.

Shipwright
Your carpentry skills will be put to use making and mending objects all around the ship.

Sailmaker
There are lots of things made from fabric on board: hammocks, awnings, stretchers, bags... As sailmaker, you will sew and repair them.

Engineer
You will be responsible for looking after HMS *Belfast*'s engines.

Captain
Your leadership skills will be vital as you command the whole crew.

THE FLOATING TOWN

17

FOOD AND DRINK

It was an old Royal Navy tradition for sailors to get a 'tot' of rum every day. Everyone apart from officers was given their rum mixed with water so that it would not keep well, to prevent them from saving it up. Sailors got around this by giving each other 'sippers' to pay back another day. On his birthday a sailor often received enough 'sippers' from his mess mates to get very drunk.

> *'I never had better grub.'*
> Stoker Larry Fursland

> *'There was an enormous tub of boiling cocoa, made by directing a hose of steam from the engine room onto raw cakes of cocoa and slabs of sugar. This made a splendid and satisfying brew.'*
> Ordinary Seaman John Wilson

Fun Fact

If you struggle with all the ladders on HMS *Belfast*, be glad that it's not your turn to be 'mess cook'. Before the canteen was built, one person from each Messdeck had to collect his mess mates' food from the Galley and bring it back on trays. wedging himself into the ladders using his knees and elbows to hold firm in rough seas. No-one wanted to drop the food.

Sailors on HMS *Furious* grab sandwiches and cocoa on deck in 1944.

FUN AND GAMES

There was time for fun as well as work on board HMS *Belfast*. When the ship was at sea the crew spent their free time playing games and sports or enjoying many other hobbies: reading, writing letters, listening to music, knitting and doing embroidery.

> *'Next to me at this mess table is an enormous hairy seaman with a great black beard making a woolly dog for his children's Christmas. It is frightfully good, but it is laughable to see him doing it.'*
>
> Ordinary Seaman John Wilson, 1943

'Crossing the line' was an old tradition to celebrate the first time someone crossed the equator. In the strange, carnival-like ceremony, members of the crew dressed up as the sea king Neptune, his queen and royal attendants. Those sailors 'crossing the line' for the first time were dunked in a tub of water.

A game of deck hockey on board HMS *Kent*.

HMS *Belfast*'s crew would often go ashore to play sports, including football, hockey, rugby, cricket and boxing. There were fierce sporting rivalries with other Royal Navy ships. At sea they played a fast game called deck hockey on the Quarterdeck. It used up a lot of pucks (balls) as they often went overboard.

Start a Conversation

Letters were often the only way to keep in touch with loved ones. To keep information from the enemy, sailors often could not say where they were, what the ship was doing or what the weather was like. What would you write home about?

King Neptune and his court on the fo'c'sle of a Royal Navy cruiser.

Uckers was a popular board game, similar to Ludo.

END OF EMPIRE 1945–1950

In August 1945 HMS *Belfast* was on its way to join the war against the Japanese in the Pacific. The ship had just arrived in Australia when the Second World War ended. Although HMS *Belfast* would no longer be fighting as planned, there was still plenty of work to do.

People visiting HMS *Belfast* for an open day in Saigon, Vietnam in 1949.

At the end of the war HMS *Belfast* was sent to Shanghai, China, which had been controlled by Japan. One of the crew's jobs was to help thousands of British civilians freed from Japanese prison camps, including many children. At the end of September 1945 the crew threw a children's party on board. Food was made by the cooks and swings and zip-wire rides were set up around the decks.

RESCUE OF REFUGEES, 1949

HMS *BELFAST* SAILED FOR PRATAS ISLAND IN THE SOUTH CHINA SEA WHERE A SHIP FULL OF CHINESE NATIONALIST REFUGEES WAS STUCK ON A REEF. THEY HAD FLED CHINESE COMMUNIST FORCES DURING THE CIVIL WAR.

CHINESE NATIONALIST LIEUTENANT-GENERAL CHOU LI-HUAN WAS ON BOARD HMS *BELFAST* TO HELP ORGANISE THE RESCUE. OVER 200 PEOPLE WERE BROUGHT ON BOARD SHIP.

THE SHIP'S COOKS TRIED TO MAKE CHINESE-STYLE MEALS FOR THE REFUGEES. HMS *BELFAST*'S CHINESE SAILORS SLEPT IN GUN TURRETS SO WOMEN AND CHILDREN COULD USE THEIR MESSDECKS.

THE REFUGEES WERE TAKEN SAFELY TO HONG KONG, FROM WHERE THEY TRAVELLED ON TO FORMOSA (TAIWAN).

HMS *Belfast* in Hong Kong harbour, 1946.

The British Empire was weaker after the Second World War. Important British colonies in Asia had been conquered by the Japanese, including Malaya (Malaysia) and Singapore. Over the next few years one of HMS *Belfast*'s most important missions was to 'show the flag', proving that Britain again had power and influence in Asia.

The Chinese Civil War was fought between the ruling Nationalists and the Chinese Communist Party. Fighting stopped during the Second World War, but began again after the war ended.

Britain supported the Nationalists, who had been allies of Britain during the Second World War. By 1949 it was clear that the Communists were winning, however, so the Royal Navy began to help Nationalists escape mainland China.

Ng Muk Kah, also known as Jenny (middle row, second from left), cleaned and painted many ships docked in Hong Kong, including HMS *Belfast*. Her team, called Jenny's Side Party, became famous among ships and their crews. In 1980 Ng Muk Kah was awarded the British Empire Medal for her work.

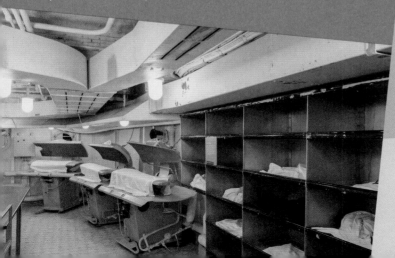

When HMS *Belfast* served in the Far East Fleet after the Second World War, many Chinese people worked alongside British sailors. Some joined the crew as part of the Navy while others worked in the ship's laundry, run as a separate business.

END OF EMPIRE 1945–1950

COLD WAR 1950–1966

The Cold War developed from a serious split between nations which had been allies in the Second World War. The UK and USA, both capitalist countries, did not trust the communist Soviet Union and feared that its influence would spread around the world. The two sides each developed nuclear weapons. The war was 'cold' because it never became a full-scale conflict between the two sides. However, Cold War tension rose as fighting broke out around the world between communist and anti-communist forces.

HMS *Belfast* firing on the enemy during the Korean War.

In 1950 HMS *Belfast* was sent to join South Korea, the USA and others who were fighting the communist North Koreans, supported by China. HMS *Belfast*'s guns were used to fire at the enemy on land. The ship's medics also treated wounded Koreans, including civilians and soldiers from both sides.

HMS BELFAST
ROLL OF HONOUR

MINING OF HMS BELFAST
PAINTER H.STANTON 30-11-39
KOREAN WAR
SERGEANT J.H.JAMES 1-3-52
CORPORAL T.R.HAMILL 1-3-52
L/STEWARD LAU SO 3-8-52

Leading Steward Lau So, from Hong Kong, was a popular member of HMS *Belfast*'s crew. Sadly he was killed in August 1952 when a North Korean shell hit his Messdeck as he slept in his hammock. Lau So was the only crew member to be killed on board the ship.

NEW THREATS

In 1952 HMS *Belfast* left Korea. By 1956 the threat from nuclear weapons had become clear and Britain was planning for new types of war. Over the next three years HMS *Belfast* was fully modernised and given:

Special air-conditioning to protect the crew from nuclear, biological and chemical weapons

Water jets to clean off radioactive substances

Improved anti-aircraft guns

SHOWING THE FLAG

By 'showing the flag' to countries in Asia, the Far East and the Caribbean, HMS *Belfast* reminded people of Britain's continuing global role and influence. The crew had a serious job to do in uncertain times, but there was also a chance for sightseeing and celebrations.

HMS *Belfast* had a Royal Marine band which played on special occasions, including when the ship was open to the public. This photo (left) shows the band playing for soldiers in Korea in 1952.

Fun Fact

To allow the crew to swim safely in the warm waters of the Pacific, the Captain bought an anti-shark swimming net. The net, made up by the Chief Sailmaker, was hung from long poles and weighted at the bottom.

HMS *Belfast* at Saigon, Vietnam, 14 December 1946. The ship is dressed with colourful flags to mark the birthday of George VI.

GUARANTEED SHARK AND SAILOR PROOF

GLOBAL TRAVELS

HMS *Belfast* sailed all over the world, seeking to strengthen and defend the power of Britain and the British Empire. The crew had to work in many different climates and conditions. For some their service took them on 'the worst journey in the world'; for others it was the tour of a lifetime.

Fun Fact

HMS *Belfast* was in service for 27 years. In that time it travelled over half a million miles.

San Francisco

VANCOUVER

BELFAST

UNITED STATES OF AMERICA
USA
USA

VANCOUVER

SAN FRANCISCO

From Hawaii

HAWAII
WELCOME TO ADVENTURE

TRINIDAD AND TOBAGO

PANAMA

TRINIDAD

ICELAND

MURMANSK

BELFAST

LONDON

MALTA

PORT SAID

ADEN

KENYA

TANZANIA

AFRICA

TANZANIA

SINGAPORE
POST OFFICE
SINGAPORE

SHANGHAI

HONG KONG

CEYLON (now SRI LANKA)

SINGAPORE

TOKYO

To

PERTH

SYDNEY

WELLINGTON

> *'We would be at sea four or five days, go in to a new port, spend two or three days in there, and then be off at sea again. So it was the best unpaid [i.e. free] cruise in the world, really.'*
> Ernie Smith, Regulating Petty Officer 1961–62, on HMS *Belfast*'s final voyage home

HMS BELFAST TIMELINE

1939 Northern Patrol, blockading enemy ships

1943–1944 Arctic Convoys

1944 D-Day landings in France

1945 Helping British civilians freed from Japanese camps

1945–1950 'Showing the flag' in Australia, New Zealand, Pacific Islands, Japan, Vietnam and Singapore

1945–1949 Chinese Civil War

1950–1952 Korean War

1959–1962 Service in the Far East — Hong Kong, Singapore and Australia — with visits to India, Ceylon (now Sri Lanka), Kenya and Tanzania

1962 HMS *Belfast*'s last voyage back to the UK

STICKER IT!

CLOTHING

The extreme environments in which HMS *Belfast*'s crew worked needed special clothing. Use your stickers to dress the sailors for the freezing Arctic and the tropical heat of the Pacific.

Arctic

Pacific

This officer on board HMS *Belfast* in 1943 is wearing a very cosy sheepskin outfit.

COMMUNICATIONS

For the crew of HMS *Belfast* to work together, and with other ships and fighting forces, they needed excellent communications. On board you can discover how communications technology changed over time, from spotter planes to radar, from voice tubes to telephones.

Large signal lamps, such as this one on the Flag Deck, were used to send messages in Morse Code to nearby ships.

ACTIVITY

HMS *Belfast*'s Wireless Office.

Wireless Operators used radios to communicate with the outside world. Morse Code turned written messages into sound by replacing each letter with a combination of long and short beeps. Wireless Operators had to learn this code by heart. Some messages were sent in secret code as well. The Operator had to get every message exactly right, even if he could not understand what it said.

> Len Beardsley was on duty in the Wireless Office a few days after D-Day when:
>
> *'I fell asleep! But I didn't know that I'd fallen asleep — all I knew was I'd missed the message. I couldn't understand it. I thought well, I must have dozed off. Four hours on four hours off, 24 hours a day, I mean crikey!'*
> Wireless Operator Len Beardsley

MORSE CODE

Use the Morse alphabet to write your name here:

A	B	C	D	E
·—	—···	—·—·	—··	·
F	**G**	**H**	**I**	**J**
··—·	——·	····	··	·———
K	**L**	**M**	**N**	**O**
—·—	·—··	——	—·	———
P	**Q**	**R**	**S**	**T**
·——·	——·—	·—·	···	—
U	**V**	**W**	**X**	**Y**	**Z**
··—	···—	·——	—··—	—·——	——··

Can you read this message?

· ·—· —— —·——

·— ·—· — —·——

—·—· ——— — ·—· ··· —·—— ·—— · —··

[In Morse Code: ENEMY LANDING CONFIRMED]

HMS *Belfast* needed to bring mail on board, as well as supplies such as food and ammunition. In a port this could be done using the cranes in the middle of the ship. At sea another method was needed: 'Replenishment At Sea', or 'RASing' for short. Two ships sailed alongside each other. They slung cables between them to pass over the goods – or even people – carefully. This photograph shows Rear Admiral AK Scott-Moncrieff travelling by cable from HMS *Belfast* to another ship.

The operators of ASDIC (commonly known as SONAR today) worked on the lowest level of the ship. ASDIC equipment sent out a 'ping' sound, then received echoes in response if the sound bounced back off an object underwater. The distinctive sound gave ASDIC Operator Bob Shrimpton his nickname of Ping.

Radar technology uses radio waves to find objects such as ships and aircraft. A transmitter sends out pulses of radio waves; when they bounce off an object and come back, the signal can reveal an object's location, size and speed. The masts in this photo held updated radar aerials, added to HMS *Belfast* in the 1950s.

'You sat in front of this little screen in a darkened room and you looked at this little tiny screen with a blue and white line across it and you were looking for what they called "echoes", little blips on the line, and the restriction was to about 20 minutes on the set because of the strain on the eyes.'
Radio Operator George Burridge

27

A MUSEUM SHIP 1971–NOW

After HMS *Belfast*'s service in the Navy ended, it became only the second Royal Navy ship to be kept as a museum ship. Although no longer in service, HMS *Belfast* still needs a hardworking crew to keep it safe and 'shipshape'. Staff and volunteers work together to look after the ship.

This Bofors anti-aircraft gun and its mount on the port side of the ship needed a lot of restoration work. The conservation team had to take the gun apart and replace some of the corroded steel, then check, restore and clean each piece. The team made a spreadsheet to keep track of all the hundreds of parts so they could fit them back together in the right order.

In 1971 HMS *Belfast* was towed up the River Thames to the spot where it still sits. This had to be done at low tide so the masts would fit under Tower Bridge.

DANGER – RUST

There is a lot of metal to keep clean on a ship the size of HMS *Belfast*. Between May 1959 and January 1961 the crew got through 6,276 tins of Bluebell brass cleaner! Today the cleaning team use about 140 tins in that amount of time.

Fun Fact

Four paid staff and around 40 volunteers work together in the conservation team. They include former Royal Navy sailors and engineers, as well as students, a motorbike mechanic and a builder of theatre sets.

The biggest threat to HMS *Belfast* these days comes from the weather. Most of the ship is made from steel, which can corrode (rust) when it touches water and oxygen.

A coating of paint protects metal from the water and oxygen, which together cause corrosion. If the paint chips off, a patch of rust can eat away a hole in the metal underneath, starting a leak.

When painters gave HMS *Belfast* a new coat of paint recently, they abseiled over the side with tins of paint clipped to their harnesses.

STICKER IT!

SMELLS ON BOARD

HMS *Belfast's* curators use smells to help visitors experience the ship as the crew did. Use your stickers to send the right aroma oil to each part of the ship.

Galley

undry

Gun Turret

6 June 1944

Sick Bay

Bakery

FOR GROWN-UPS

▶ HMS *Belfast* is a historic site, with uneven floors and awkward spaces. Your group will need to learn how to move around the ship safely, just as the sailors who served on board did. Make sure that everyone knows to face ladders when they climb up or down and to mind their feet (and heads, for those tall enough) as they go through doors and hatches.

▶ The Engine and Boiler Rooms are not suitable for children under 1.2m (4ft) tall due to vertical ladders and narrow walkways.

▶ Use the map in this book and others available from our quayside pavilion to find your way around — but do not worry too much. The layout of the ship can be confusing and getting lost is part of the fun. If you need help, friendly Yeomen (people who look after the ship) and volunteers on board will be happy to help you get your bearings.

▶ You will find plenty of opportunities to get hands-on with the ship as you explore. Take a seat in the Captain's chair or pull up a bench in the Messdeck; read through real letters and diaries or play the sailors' favourite board game, Uckers.

▶ HMS *Belfast* was an active warship which served in conflict. Some of the stories you may encounter on board, for instance in the Sick Bay, deal with the grim realities of war and some traumatic experiences. If your children are upset by what they see on board, you may want to find a quiet space to talk about it later on.

▶ Kids' lunch bags are available in our café, together with sandwiches, snacks and hot and cold drinks.

▶ The Main Deck, Quarterdeck, Boat Deck and café have been adapted to be accessible to wheelchairs, pushchairs and buggies. Other parts of the ship are unfortunately not accessible for visitors on wheels.

▶ Baby changing facilities are available in the toilets on the Main Deck.

OTHER IWM BRANCHES

We hope you enjoyed your visit to HMS *Belfast*. For more days out exploring IWM'S collections, head to our other museums.

IWM NORTH

IWM's home in Manchester is housed in a dramatic building which represents how war disrupts the world. Its exhibitions tell stories from conflicts since the First World War. Immerse yourself in the 360° cinematic Big Picture Show and see the *Poppies* display.

IWM LONDON

IWM London tells the story of people's experiences of war, from the First World War to today. There are countless discoveries to be made across its six floors and through its free family activities.

IWM DUXFORD

Prepare for a huge day out at IWM Duxford — Europe's largest air museum. See planes take to the sky from the airfield where Spitfires first flew. Get up close to over a century of aviation with hundreds of planes, vehicles, boats and more!

CHURCHILL WAR ROOMS

This is the underground bunker in Central London where Churchill's government worked during the Blitz. Find out how the Cabinet operated here in secret from 1940 to 1945, and visit the museum dedicated to Prime Minister Winston Churchill.

Published by IWM, Lambeth Road, London SE1 6HZ
1st edition, 2022
© The Trustees of the Imperial War Museum, 2022

ISBN: 978-1-912423-52-1
Printed by Belmont Press, UK

The publishers will be glad to make good in future editions any error or omissions brought to their attention.

Our thanks to Jo Foster (author), GBL Studios (design), Frances Castle (comic strip illustrations), Darren Baxter (front cover illustration and drawing on p. 23), Catherine Bradley (project manager) and all IWM staff involved in this book.

NAUTICAL WORDSEARCH

Find these words you might need on board ship. They might read up, down, right, left or diagonally. Sailors on HMS *Belfast* regularly used words such as these.

B	N	E	D	R	W	V	E	S	S	E	M
J	R	O	E	M	Y	A	H	F	F	G	K
S	E	G	C	B	L	G	T	I	N	P	E
E	T	B	K	S	A	W	N	Y	H	L	S
L	S	A	N	W	R	S	H	I	A	L	N
L	T	M	R	O	P	U	D	E	T	G	M
M	R	C	I	B	T	E	G	O	C	A	T
E	V	H	T	R	O	P	H	N	H	W	R
E	S	D	G	N	O	A	B	L	R	K	E
H	U	L	L	B	C	U	R	G	A	F	L
C	E	B	R	T	H	E	A	D	S	I	L
Y	H	T	O	Y	I	L	E	B	H	O	K

BOW – the front of a ship

DECK – a floor or level of a ship

HATCH RASH – an injury to the shin from doors or ladders

HEADS – toilets

HULL – the main body of a ship

MESS – the place where sailors eat and drink

PORT – the left-hand side of a ship

RATING – a sailor below officer rank

STARBOARD – the right-hand side of a ship

STERN – the back of a ship

Pacific

Arctic

Cordite

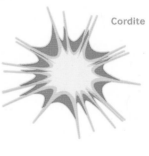